Build a Weather Station

BY CAROL HAND · ILLUSTRATED BY ROGER STEWART

The Child's World®
childsworld.com

Published by The Child's World®
1980 Lookout Drive · Mankato, MN 56003-1705
800-599-READ · www.childsworld.com

Acknowledgments
The Child's World®: Mary Swensen, Publishing Director
Red Line Editorial: Editorial direction and production
The Design Lab: Design

Photographs ©: Shutterstock Images, 4; T.W. van Urk/
Shutterstock Images, 5; iStockphoto, 6

Design Elements: JosephTodaro/Texturevault; Shutterstock Images

ISBN 9781503807891

LCCN 2015919408

Printed in the United States of America
Mankato, MN
June, 2016
PA02301

ABOUT THE AUTHOR

Carol Hand is a science writer. She has written a number of books on weather, climate, and the environment for young people.

ABOUT THE ILLUSTRATOR

Roger Stewart has been an artist and illustrator for more than 30 years. His first job involved drawing aircraft parts. Since then, he has worked in advertising, design, film, and publishing. Roger has lived in London, England, and Sydney, Australia, but he now lives on the southern coast of England.

Contents

CHAPTER ONE
MEASURING WEATHER, 4

CHAPTER TWO
PREDICTING CHANGES, 6

CHAPTER THREE
BUILDING A WEATHER STATION, 8

Glossary, 22

To Learn More, 23

Index, 24

Measuring Weather

Weather is all the outside conditions in a place from day to day. Is it warm or cold? Is it sunny or cloudy? Is it windy or still? Climate is average weather. It describes what weather has been like in a place over many years.

Weather has many features. One feature is temperature, or how hot or cold it is. We measure temperature with a **thermometer**. Another feature is precipitation, or water falling from the sky. It may fall as rain, snow, or sleet. We measure rain with a rain gauge. The rain gauge collects rain. It measures the amount in inches or centimeters.

People can use thermometers to help decide how to dress.

Wind is also part of weather. Wind is moving air. In a tornado, wind moves very fast. In a breeze, it moves slowly. We measure wind speed using an **anemometer**. Wind spins an anemometer's arms in circles. The device measures how fast the arms spin. This gives the wind speed. We measure wind direction using a wind vane. A wind vane points in the direction the wind is blowing.

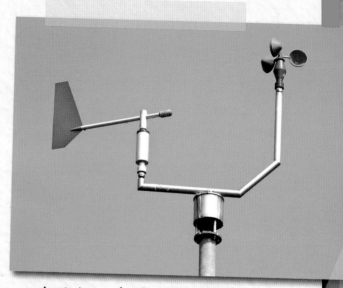

A wind vane (left) and an anemometer (right) measure wind direction and speed.

Another part of weather is air pressure. Air pressure tells when a storm is coming. An instrument called a **barometer** measures air pressure. Weather stations have these instruments. People use them to measure climate and predict weather. People who study weather and climate are called meteorologists.

CHAPTER TWO

Predicting Changes

Weather is always changing. Energy from the sun creates winds on Earth. This moves heat and water around the planet. The movement changes the weather. Temperatures rise and fall. Storms roll in and pass by.

Weather affects many things. It might affect whether you go outside or whether you wear a jacket. You don't need to measure weather to make these choices. You can feel the

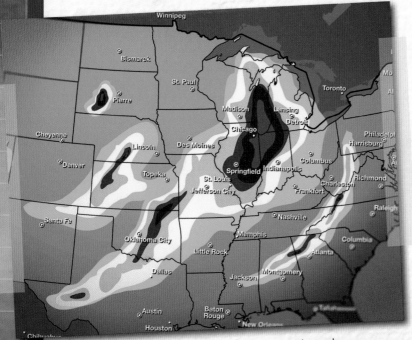

Meteorologists use technology to track and predict changes in weather.

temperature or see the rain. But many people need to know more about weather. Farmers must plan when to plant and **harvest** crops. Bad weather can hurt crops. This causes farmers to lose money. Fishermen must know about coming storms. People who run ski resorts must predict snow. People who live along coasts must know when **hurricanes** are nearing. Anyone who transports people or things must pay attention to weather. Storms or floods can make travel dangerous. Big storms can affect all of us. We need to know when they will reach us. We need to know how strong they will be.

Meteorologists track bad weather. They help people know what to expect. These scientists also learn about climate. They keep careful records over many years. You too can pay attention to weather and climate. Paying attention can help you be ready for anything nature throws your way.

LONG-TERM CHANGES

The world's climate is getting warmer. Burning fuels such as coal, oil, and gas speeds up warming. Many people try to help slow **global warming**. They ride in cars less. They walk or ride their bicycles instead. Some people wear warmer clothes indoors instead of turning up the heat.

CHAPTER THREE

Building a Weather Station

RAIN GAUGE

You can make a rain gauge to add to your station. Take a glass, jar, or tube. Measure 3.75 teaspoons (18 mL) of water. Pour it into the glass. Put a line at the water level. Label it 1 inch (2.5 cm). Add another 3.75 teaspoons (18 mL). Label it 2 inches (5 cm). Continue making marks until you cannot add any more water. Empty the rain gauge. Leave it in an open space outdoors. Check the rain gauge after it rains. Record the number of inches. Then, empty it.

You can make your own weather station. You can bring it outside when you want to take measurements. Record your results in a notebook. The readings can help you notice patterns. This will help you learn about the climate and weather in your area. You may also be able to predict bad weather. Compare your results to your local weather **forecast**.

You can use everyday materials to make your station. Find a place to work. Gather your materials. As you work, ask an adult for help when you need it. Let's get started!

MATERIALS

Wind Vane

- [ ] Scissors
- [ ] Heavy paper or cardstock
- [ ] Ruler
- [ ] Masking tape
- [ ] 12-inch (30 cm) drinking straw
- [ ] Straight pin
- [ ] Pencil with eraser

Anemometer

- [ ] Scissors
- [ ] 5 3-ounce paper cups
- [ ] 2 12-inch (30 cm) drinking straws
- [ ] Stapler
- [ ] Straight pin
- [ ] Pencil with eraser

Barometer

- [ ] Mason jar or tall glass
- [ ] Balloon
- [ ] Scissors
- [ ] Rubber band
- [ ] 12-inch (30 cm) drinking straw
- [ ] Masking tape
- [ ] Sheet of plain 8.5 x 11 inch (22 x 28 cm) paper
- [ ] Pen

Weather Station

- [ ] Large cardboard box without lid at least 14 inches (36 cm) wide and 11 inches (28 cm) tall
- [ ] Thermometer

WIND VANE INSTRUCTIONS

STEP 1: Take the scissors. Cut out a 4-inch (10 cm) square of cardstock.

STEP 2: Take the 4-inch (10 cm) square of card stock. Use a ruler to draw a **diagonal** line. Cut along the line to make two triangles.

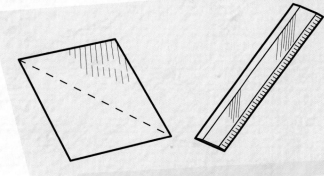

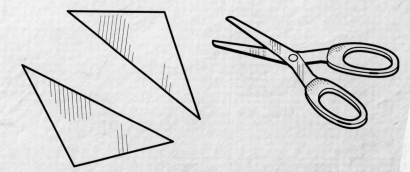

STEP 3: Tape a triangle to the last inch (2.5 cm) of each end of the straw. The triangles should point in the same direction.

STEP 4: Push the pin through the straw at its center. Then push the pin into the eraser of the pencil. Set the wind vane aside.

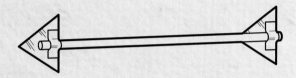

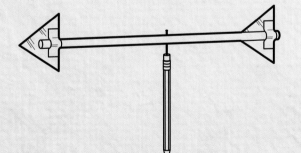

ANEMOMETER INSTRUCTIONS

STEP 1: Take a cup. Using the scissors, make a hole in the middle of one of the sides.

STEP 2: Push the straw through the hole.

STEP 3: Flatten the end of the straw inside the cup. Staple it to the opposite side of the cup.

STEP 4: Repeat Steps 2 and 3 with a second cup and straw.

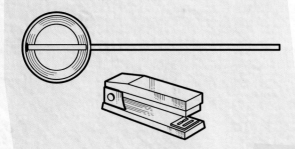

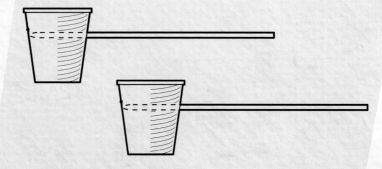

STEP 5: Take a third cup. Use the scissors to make four holes. Have an adult help. The holes should be at least halfway up from the bottom of the cup. They should be spaced equally around the outside of the cup. Make a fifth hole in bottom of the cup.

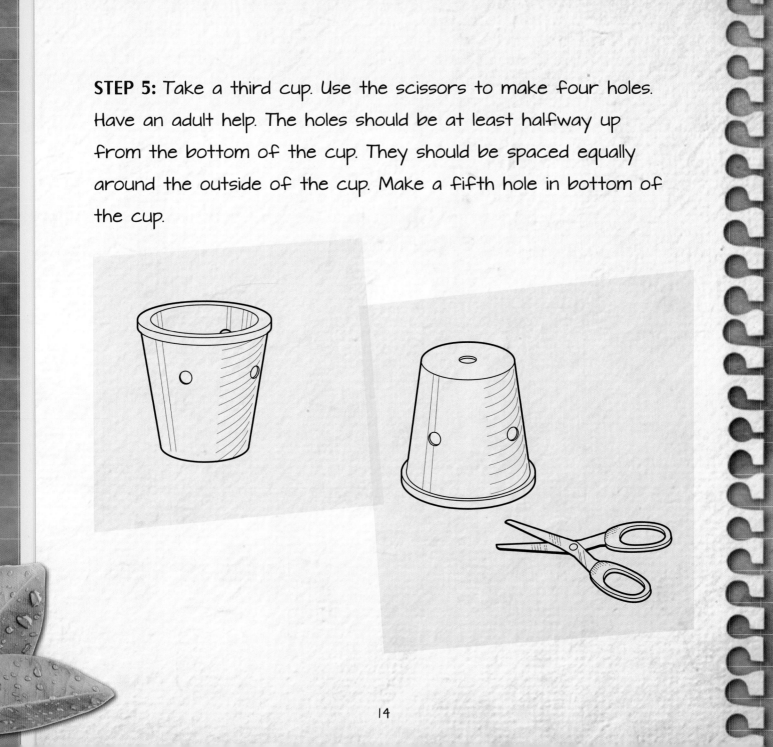

STEP 6: Push the two straws through two opposite holes in the five-hole cup. The straws should cross inside the cup.

STEP 7: Add a second cup to the other end of each straw. The open end of each cup should face the bottom of the one in front of it. Use the stapler to attach the cups.

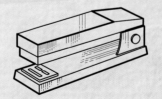

STEP 8: Push the pin through where the two straws cross. Push the eraser end of the pencil through the hole in the bottom of the middle cup. Stick the pin into the eraser. Set the anemometer aside.

BAROMETER INSTRUCTIONS

STEP 1: Take the balloon. Blow it up to stretch it out. Release the air. Take the scissors. Cut off the narrow part of the balloon.

STEP 2: Place the wide part of the balloon over the top of the jar. Make sure it fits tightly. Put the rubber band around the neck of the jar. It will hold the balloon in place.

STEP 3: Take the straw. Tape it to the balloon lid. One inch (2.5 cm) of the straw should sit on top of the jar. The rest should hang off the edge.

STEP 4: Take the piece of paper. Using a ruler, draw a line every inch (2.5 cm) going up. At the top of the scale, write "High." Write "Low" at the bottom.

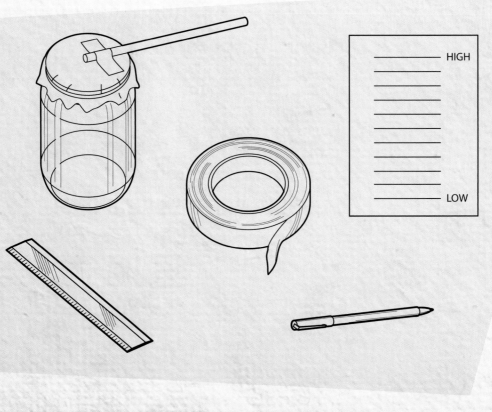

WEATHER STATION INSTRUCTIONS

MEASURING

With your station put together, you can start recording the weather. Look at the barometer. If the pressure is high, the weather will tend to be fair. If it drops down, clouds and rain are likely. Use a compass to tell you which way the wind vane points. Use a timer for the anemometer. Count how many times it spins in one minute. You can draw an X on one of the cups. Use the X to mark each turn. Record your measurements in your notebook.

STEP 1: Tape the paper scale to the inside back wall of the box.

STEP 2: Place the barometer in the box. The end of the straw should sit in front of the scale.

STEP 3: Tape the thermometer to the bottom of the box. Do not cover the bulb at the bottom.

STEP 4: Take the anemometer and wind vane. Stick their pencils into opposite ends of the box. They should stick out of the top. Tape the bottom of the pencil to the inside wall of the box.

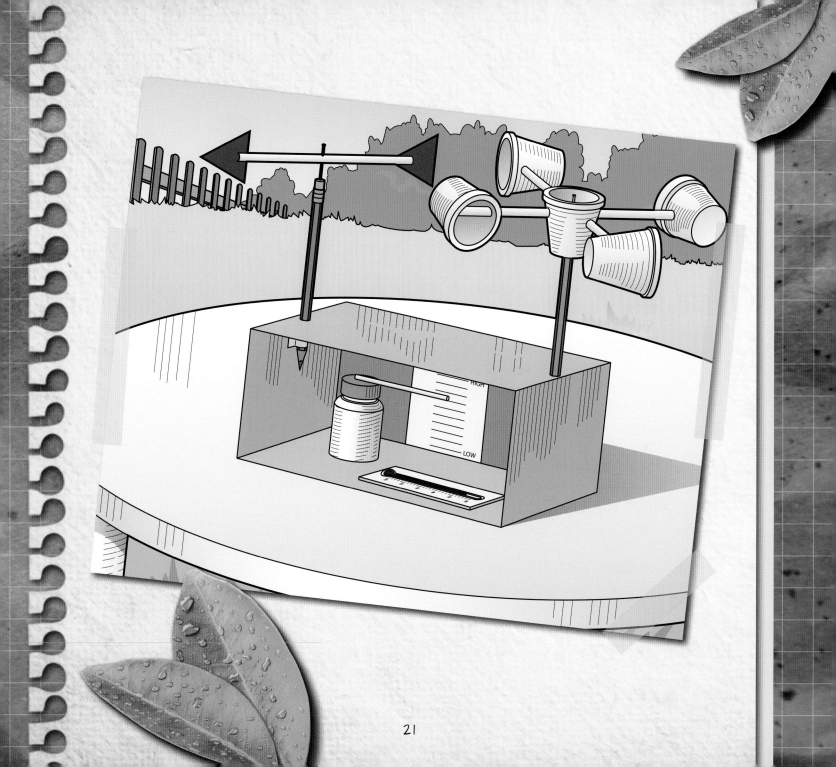

GLOSSARY

anemometer (an-i-MAH-mi-tur) An anemometer is an instrument used to measure the wind's speed. Wind spins an anemometer.

barometer (buh-RAH-mi-tur) A barometer is an instrument used to measure air pressure. A barometer can help predict weather.

diagonal (dye-AG-uh-nul) A diagonal line is a line from one corner of a square or rectangle to the opposite corner. Diagonal lines travel at a slant.

forecast (FOR-kast) A forecast is a prediction about what will happen in the future. A meteorologist gives a weather forecast.

global warming (GLOH-bul WOR-ming) Global warming is the rise in temperature of the world's climate. Global warming increases when humans burn fossil fuels.

harvest (HAR-vist) To harvest is to gather crops that are ripe. Farmers use big machines to harvest their crops.

hurricanes (HUR-i-kanes) Hurricanes are storms with very strong rotating winds. Hurricanes form over warm oceans.

thermometer (thur-MAH-mi-tur) A thermometer is an instrument used to measure temperature. The mercury in a thermometer rises and falls based on the temperature.

TO LEARN MORE

In the Library

Breen, Mark, and Kathleen Friestad. *The Kids' Book of Weather*. Nashville, TN: Ideals, 2008.

Furgang, Kathy. *National Geographic Kids Everything Weather: Facts, Photos, and Fun that Will Blow You Away*. Washington, DC: National Geographic Children's, 2012.

Snedeker, Joe. *The Everything KIDS' Weather Book*. Avon, MA: Adams Media, 2012.

Taylor-Butler, Christine. *Meteorology: The Study of Weather*. New York: Scholastic, 2012.

On the Web

Visit our Web site for links about weather stations:
childsworld.com/links

Note to Parents, Teachers, and Librarians: We routinely verify our Web links to make sure they are safe and active sites. So encourage your readers to check them out!

INDEX

air pressure, 5
anemometer, 5, 9, 17, 20

barometer, 5, 9, 20
breeze, 5

climate, 4-5, 7, 8
compass, 20

diagonal, 10

energy, 6

farmer, 7
fishermen, 7
flood, 7
forecast, 8
fuel, 7

global warming, 7

harvest, 7
hurricane, 7

meteorologist, 5, 7

notebook, 8, 20

precipitation, 4
prediction, 5, 7, 8

rain gauge, 4, 8

storm, 5, 6-7

temperature, 4, 6-7
thermometer, 4, 9, 20
tornado, 5

weather, 4-5, 6-7, 8, 20
wind, 4-5, 6
wind vane, 5, 11, 20